My State of
Felicity

Angelina Schreiber

3rd birthday edition! ♡

Bibliografische Information der Deutschen
Nationalbibliothek: Die Deutsche Nationalbibliothek
verzeichnet diese Publikation in der Deutschen
Nationalbibliografie; detaillierte bibliografische Daten sind
im Internet über http://dnb.dnb.de abrufbar.

© 2025 Angelina Schreiber
Verlag: BoD · Books on Demand GmbH, Überseering 33,
22297 Hamburg, bod@bod.de
Druck: Libri Plureos GmbH, Friedensallee 273,
22763 Hamburg
ISBN: 978-3-8192-1210-9

To my friends Linda & Nele,
my cousin Victoria,
& my past me

Angelina Schreiber

Let me tell you the story
about finding the place
where your soul will
forever find its peace.

Get yourself some rest
& let my words guide you through
darkness, growth and felicity.

My State of Felicity

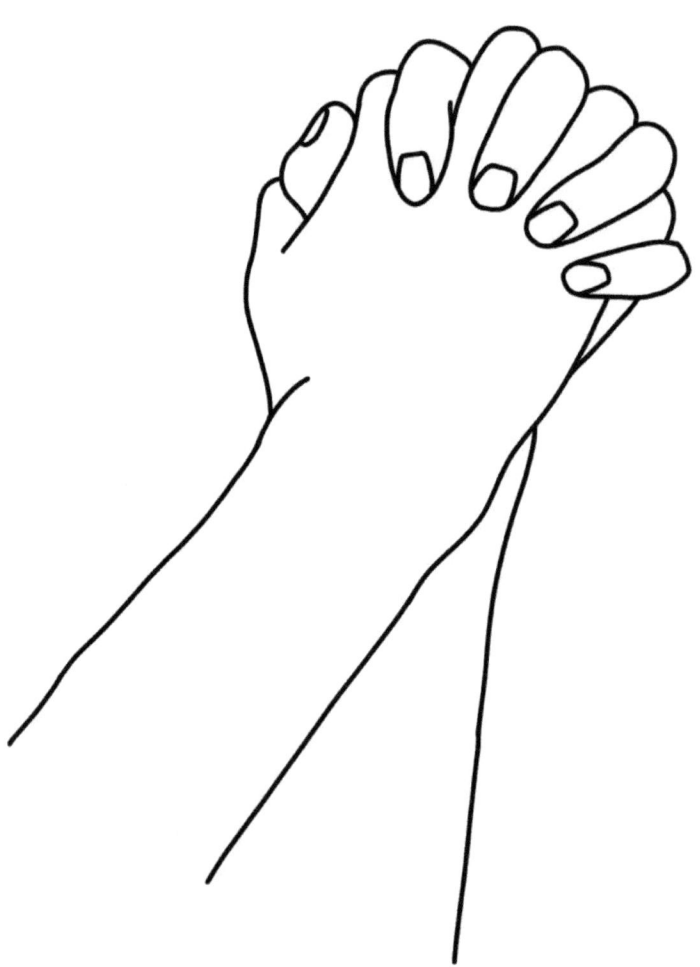

Darkness · noun
[dahrk•nis] pl. darknesses

This marks a gloomy and depressed state of life.
An individual may feel empty and sad,
thinking their emotions are overwhelming
them to the fullest.

There is darkness
everywhere I go

— I am afraid of the dark

A whirlwind swept over my life
causing too much pain,
changing me into the person
I never wanted to be.

– chaotic, with a pinch of disorientation

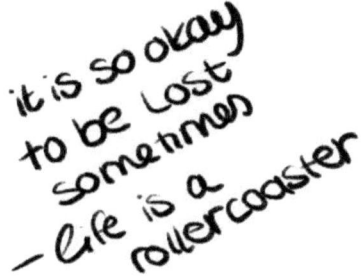

it is so okay
to be lost
sometimes
– life is a
rollercoaster

The person in the mirror turns out to be
my biggest enemy in this battle of life.

Angelina Schreiber

I cannot tell you how many times
I laid in my bed, in regret of always saying
I was alright even though I wasn´t.

– trapped in my own four walls

My State of Felicity

Let me show you how cruel
the society can be to a person:

Your mind spills art, honey.
And you are afraid to show it
to the world.

Them saying that I would not make it
made me believe that my life was created
for me to fail.

prove them
wrong!

Oppression is telling a sunflower
in a field of roses to fit in
and stop behaving like herself.

– this is how you make me feel

And while I was trying to cure the panic
inside of me, the only thing I could hear
was myself breaking down.

– helpless

To-Do list for everyday of the week:
1.   Find 5 things I can see
2.   Find 4 things I can feel
3.   Find 3 things I can hear
4.   Find 2 things I can smell
5.   Find 1 thing I can taste

– it will never stop to be significant, will it?

And my tears are rolling down
symbolizing the tragedy of a dying plant.

– I am a lost & wild flower

My State of Felicity

Glass shattered.
A million pieces on the ground.
Not even the moments that mattered,
would keep me away from getting drowned.

– my own expectations

Procrastination seemed like the right thing to do,
until the regret came in like the flu.

– slowly, getting heavier step by step

My State of Felicity

All I see is a broken, hardly spoken to little girl.
Whose wings needed to go through too much at her age.
Afraid of falling, lost her trust.
All she did was crawling in the dust.

Angelina Schreiber

The most meaningful words were left unsaid.
Shattering the deepest parts of my soul.
Thinking about how I will never feel ready to be repaired.

My State of Felicity

You told me that you would be
by my side until the end of the line.
Great to know that your line
once split itself from mine.

Angelina Schreiber

The place where you used to be is shadowed,
waiting for someone to turn on the light.

After all, it was just a poem in my head.
Nothing more to worry about.

& as soon as our paths split up,
all I wanted to say is:
I hate you
      I hate you
           I hate you
               I hate you
                    I miss you

My State of Felicity

Your voice remained silence.
The world's moving in stop-motion.
It feels like violence.
And drowning in an ocean.
Full of loss, emptiness & hurt.

The sun grew cold and the light went missing
as soon as you left us.

– how should we live without you?

My State of Felicity

You made living in my shelter so easy,
even though I could not make it out there alone.
I thought that you would give me your hand,
or you would just stand by my side.

The truth is, you were just there
to dig my hole deeper
to let me suffer down here alone.

At the end, I was not in love with you,
I was in love with the thought of you.

Sometimes we
are not in love
with the person,
sometimes we are
just in love with
the version of
them we created
in our head.

TOUCH PART I

The hands that once touched me
were too familiar and warm,
they had this kind of charm.

Were never afraid,
never needed a break,
they always stayed.

Until this day, where I needed to pray.
Everything turned dark,
he gave me this mark, in my heart.

And then he went away,
making everything grey.

Leaving me alone,
while he stepped onto his throne,
forgetting who helped him
when his leg was stuck under a heavy stone.

The hands that once touched m
 made me believe that I was the thief of his relief.

My State of Felicity

I was the yellow dye
painting the stars, the flowers,
the sun and moon on the canvas.

But, oh my,
you could only see
in black and white.

– making me feel so not worth it

Angelina Schreiber

In this relationship,
I did not only show you my body.
I showed you my bare-naked soul,
which was way harder for me.
And you knew,
but you only kept abusing my thoughts
to get more of my body.

– the shame is all on you

almost
like her,
enough for you

– a six-word tragedy

"Will you write a poem about me?",
he asked me silently.

And I thought about it for hours until I came to the solution that indeed I will. Somewhere between all the fear, hate and mostly pain you still mattered. And I keep telling myself that the only thing I will ever feel for you is hate. The truth is, somewhere deep down, there is still a feeling that aches for an embrace and peace. And that is what I hate the most.

My State of Felicity

You making my forest burn.

That's when I had to learn,
that the feeling of never healing
from a parent
that forever stopped caring about their child
will stay way further than the day
their childhood days will be left behind.

With a heart that wished for a restart.
Hoping that their love will finally take a part.

Angelina Schreiber

At some point the crying just stops.
And all that is left behind is an empty body
with a heart that screams for recognition.

My State of Felicity

When loved people suffer,
it breaks you,
bit by bit,
until the moment
you can´t anymore.

Angelina Schreiber

Lost lights luminate,
lost lights live alone,
lost lights were left loveless,
that's what makes them so strong.

Growth · noun
[grohth] pl. growths

The process of changing in a positive and mature way.
An individual tries to understand their past
and is on a good way to process everything
that has happened in their past.

My State of Felicity

I was standing in the shadow
of the most beautiful flower in this world.
I just had to look up.

My State of Felicity

With every sob I shed,
I was watering the seeds
of the very best moments
that were about to come.

Angelina Schreiber

You will survive the biggest storm
with nothing but trust within yourself.
Remember this.

You ripped out my heart, tore it into a million pieces & all that you repeatedly said was that I will never find a love like yours. And until this day I am not sure if you realized, but that is exactly my plan. To find someone that truly loves me and my imperfections, not somebody that just pretends.

TOUCH PART II

The hands that once touched me
weren't worth the wait
of hoping he would come back.

The hands that once touched me
stopped to matter
as soon as you came by.
With a touch so magical,
nobody had to try
comparing and ask themselves why?

You opened my eyes,
deleted my why's,
showing me that all he did was telling lies.

You touched me
like an artist would touch a masterpiece,
carefully brushing your brush upon my scars,
stopping my inner wars,
creating the most magical painting ever.

Oh you,
the person that made you believe that you are hard to love was not capable of such a soul like yours. You will surely meet someone that knows exactly how to treat a love like yours.
I promise.

the right person
will know how
to love you!
without hesitation!

Angelina Schreiber

I wanted to leave this world
without hesitation
until you showed me
that everything glows
in a different shade of yellow.

– that's when I realized

It´s not your job to create them
a life they want to live in.

– your voice matters

Angelina Schreiber

It´s not your fault if they are not
pleased with the life, they live in.

– theirs don´t

Blue was admiring yellow because it always looks so easy when yellow does it. Yellow never complains, yellow never cries, yellow always shines. But what blue does not know is that even yellow feels kind of blue sometimes.

And in this world, it never matters how the butterfly looks. We always accept them as the most beautiful beings in this world. Even with broken or unstable wings, they look so precious.

– start treating people like this

You kept breaking your own heart
with the thought of wanting to be enough
in this world.

– stop, don´t

This journey was not a straight line at all and I would not want it to be one. Because a rollercoaster without the craziest twirls and loops can´t show you all the different sides and aspects of this experience.

Do not try to avoid all the turns you will make, the feeling you will get inside of it. It will shape you, strengthen you and above all, it will prepare you for the next ride you will take.

– growth is a rollercoaster

A bee is not capable of flying around
and dusting their magic out there
without a pair of healed wings.

So, remember, before you grow
heal the damaged spots
in your heart and soul.

But with you leaving,
there came the love for the sky.
Remembering that up there high,
I can always rely on your watching eye.

a sunset is a
loved one in
heaven, telling
you they love
you! ♡

He will give me everything
I need to survive & will take everything
from me that holds me down.

– god will give me signs, like he always did

My State of Felicity

Growth is realizing
that all of the bad moments
and pain that kept you down,
weren´t your fault.

Angelina Schreiber

Growth is looking into the mirror
& screaming "I love you!"
at the top of my lungs.

"You are a sunflower without your petals.", he said looking at me. Being serious, he was right. I spent most of my life letting my head hang & every beautiful yellow petal fell to the ground. I spent my days searching for the sun in dark and shadowed places. But I also spent hours of trying to figure out that in order to bloom into the most beautiful creature on this planet, you need to keep your head high. Don´t search for sunlight in places that are dark, raise your head and witness every shine you can get!

Angelina Schreiber

You need to realize that
you will never be good enough
in their eyes.
Be good enough in yours.
Because exactly those eyes
will be looking at the reflection
of yourself for a long time from now on.

Do not let yourself be reduced
on a former lover,
who was just a chapter in your book,
that is worth thousands of appreciations.

Angelina Schreiber

Mark these words I am about to say:
If an ex-partner does not
encounter you with respect,
then they do not deserve your recognition
at all.

My State of Felicity

You are the poet of your own story.
Make those verses scream:

I deserve everything I achieved and will achieve.

Show them that you will dance
on the scars they left on you
seeding so many flowers
they get jealous of leaving you,
not knowing what you are capable of.

– you will do it just on your own

I will forever carry you in my heart, lost seed.
I will water you with my poetic words.
I will bring you to the warm & shining sun.
I will show you to the most magical bees.
I will keep you safe.
You will bloom there.

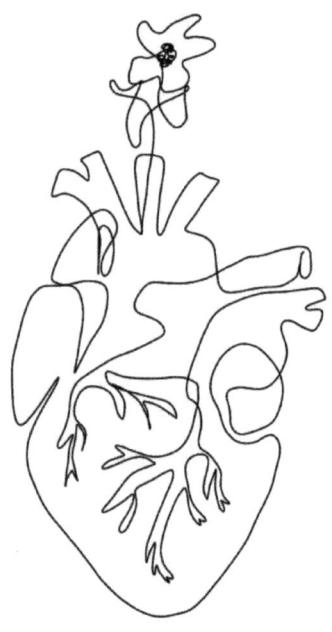

I know that a crack in the deepest part of your heart seems like the end. But always remember, if you stop trying to fill this deep hole with nonsense and allow yourself to rest, your body will thank you with beautiful flowers that will bloom out there to cure your heart.

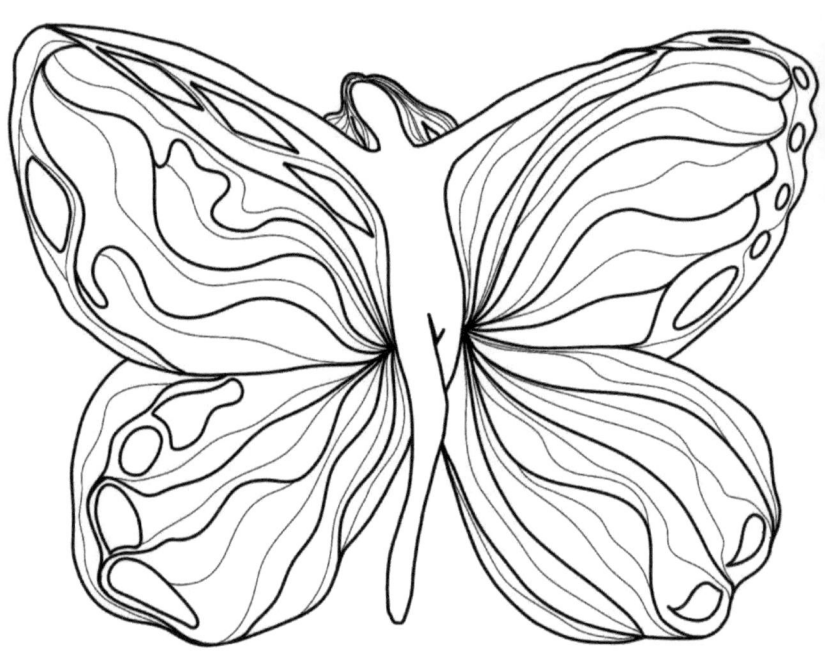

And just like the caterpillar
turns out the be
one of the most breathtaking creatures ever
I want to grow as much as it did,
making my scars turn into butterflies.

Working together with children from so many different cultural backgrounds kept inspiring me day and night. I am so amazed that they can always be themselves in a world where everyone wants to fit in so badly.

– take them as your idols, they know that they belong here

I want to tell you in Morse,
the things everybody ignores.
You need to:

• • • • / • • — / • — • / —
hurt

• • • • / — — — / • — — • / •
hope

• • • • / • / • — / • — • •
Heal

Felicity • noun
[fe•lis•i•ty] pl. felicities

This is another word for a state of happiness.
For example, you might find yourself
in a State of Felicity
the next time you are surrounded by people
or things you love or the things that inspire you.

Spending time with myself
was my way of discovering
who I want to be.

– self acceptance

Angelina Schreiber

And for the first time in my life
I do not want to please someone.
I just wanted to create something for myself.

My State of Felicity

Let´s seed happiness everywhere we go
and make this world turn itself to the sun.

It just feels like a really good poem.

Breathe, and listen to the things your body and heart want to tell you. They want to send love letters to you, appreciating everything you did for them in the good and in the bad. They know that they are not that lovable, but they stayed. And there is nothing more to be proud of.

Angelina Schreiber

Dear heart,

I know it wasn´t always easy for us two,
but I love the composition of us two,
I love the familiar feeling of us two
& most of all I love that you are not perfect.

Yours, me

My State of Felicity

I want to dance through the flower garden
of strength, hope and positivity.

Swinging around with gladioluses,
whose leaves are shaped like swords
defending themselves when times get hard.

Swirling around with yellow tulips,
which bring a bright smile on everyone´s faces.

Twirling around with sunflowers
since they will always find the way to light.

My State of Felicity

May the sea kiss your skin
and carry you on their waves,
because you are made out of foam
from the sea like Aphrodite was.

I am the person worth fighting for.

My State of Felicity

He put the stars on my ceiling
showing me that his whole world
was rotating around my mother and I.

He did not make me feel
like a moon surrounded by many more.

He makes me feel
like I am the sun
turning everything warm and comfy.

– step **dad**

Angelina Schreiber

Without crying the sky
wouldn´t be able to look down
at all the possibilities of growth.

poetry is pulling out my sadness in waves

And after years I came back to my tiny bench to write. The cold wind is blowing against my hair, bringing back all the memories, like waves bring tiny shells to the beach for kids to pick them up to create something with them or just to keep them to their selves. Today I came back, not to keep my memories to myself. I came back to create beautiful written pieces with them.

The trees are waving with their crowns welcoming me back to the place where I used to come to when I needed some time off. And the sky started to cry with me because it was not ready to let me move on, but I am. I really want to. I want to let go of all the bad things to make room for happy ones. Nevertheless, I will come back, to tell the sky about everything, because I will always have a sensitive spot for this place.

The love to yourself can move mountains.

Angelina Schreiber

Listen carefully!

The birds are singing a song to you,
because your soul is beautiful
in a way no one understands.

My State of Felicity

You belong to this world
like the sun and the rain belong
to its flowers.

Even though it´s controversial,
even though it does not feel like it.
You belong here!

– my love letter to you

Angelina Schreiber

You matter,
in every language I speak:
– you matter
– ты очень важен
– du bist wichtig
– tu es important

My State of Felicity

May your scars embellish
your beautiful skin
and won't hold you back
from telling your magical stories.

You are coloring the sky in different shades of bright orange for us to know that you are forever taking part at family dinners, vacations, birthdays, Christmas parties, graduations, weddings and so much more.

– always by our side, in thoughts

Talk to me in poetry.
Make me feel yellow.

Angelina Schreiber

Surround yourself with people
that keep watering your soul
and will seed themselves beside you,
staying when there is no sun in the sky,
and at the same time when you grow
and bloom to your fullest.

Angelina Schreiber

Look at them still witnessing
every spark of light,
even though their time is almost over.

– may the sunflowers lead you in the right direction

And they cry in their strong embrace,
because the young one couldn't be prouder
to see the old one still standing as tall as possible,

while the old one is so hurt to see
what the young one needs to go through
at some point.

But either way,
they are so glad
that they belong to each other.

– the moment your younger & older self meet again

You deserve your own warmth,
respect and love.

– take a moment to hug yourself

Me wrapping my Christmas presents
as wild as possible happens on purpose,
to show that not so perfect things
can be beautiful on the inside.

Shine like nobody´s watching –
for Y O U R S E L F

You are breathtaking.
Everything about you
is composed so beautifully.
Every freckle, every birthmark,
every stretch mark, every scar,
It belongs to your body
like every brushstroke belongs to a painting.

You are you.

At the end of the day the only thing you need to believe is that you are you. You are everything to adore and a piece in the museum called "life". I hope that you will never forget who you really are & what you deserve. By visiting some more museums, you will experience the moment of knowing that even wild things can be breathtaking at some point. Create or buy yourself some paintings that inspire you the most, to remind you that you belong into a museum, because you are art. Your soul spills so many beautiful things that make you look so divine. And even though you can´t help to be emotional sometimes, you glow like a rainbow, your heart & soul are made out of so many different colors it makes everyone speechless. They want to send so many love letters to you, you are so aesthetic. They can´t get enough of you. And as soon as you look into the mirror, I hope you find yourself grateful about every brushstroke & detail you are made of. I hope you encounter people with the same joy as you encounter yourself in the mirror. Show people who think that they are too little that they are enough for the world, because they are the most surreal and stunning painting in this universe.

My State of Felicity

I turned out to be my hairbrush song,
my Sunday afternoon,
my coffee date, my pretty self,
my comfort person, my morning sun.

My e n o u g h

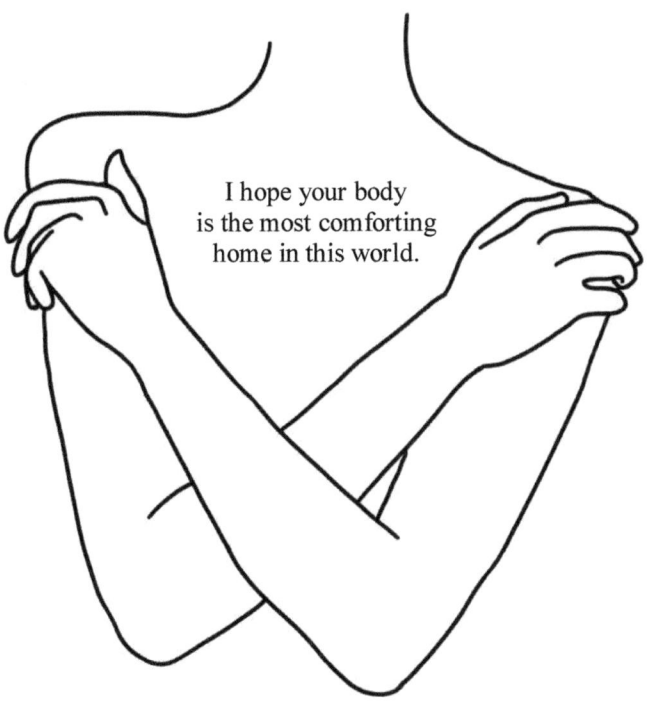

I hope your body
is the most comforting
home in this world.

2am – 2pm
Either way, I finally feel
like my soul found its peace

222
Rest.
You are on the right path.
At the right time.
In the right place.

My State of Felicity

After all of these struggles,
my life led me to my own
beautiful eucatastrophe.
– an unexpected, sudden happy ending

Angelina Schreiber

The end of this journey brings clarity.
Finding my own State of Felicity
made me seed a sunflower of hope,
love and trust within myself
as I learn to take care of them just on my own.

Angelina Schreiber

*More poems
(My State of Felicity's Version)*

My State of Felicity

You are the poem I didn't know I was writing,
the lines I'd been longing to find.
In you, I see something I didn't know could be real,
a story I want to hold onto,
a love worth every word.

Angelina Schreiber

Either you will be my forever love story,
the one I tell with stars in my eyes,
the one that feels like a home
I never want to leave,
Or you will be my greatest heartbreak,
the kind that shatters me
in ways I can't yet imagine,
leaving echoes where your love once lived.

In moments like this,
I wish you were still here,
walking this earth,
so I could show you,
Show you the life I've built,
the dreams I'm living,
the ones I used to talk about with stars in my eyes
when you were near.
I wish I could share this joy with you,
let you see how far I've come,
how the pieces of my heart
have turned into something whole.
Because no matter how much time passes,
a part of me will always want
to make you proud.

Angelina Schreiber

For years, I tried to fit
with pieces that didn't match,
forcing edges, breaking corners,
losing parts of myself in the process.

My State of Felicity

What if you still search for the mosaic of her in me,
pieces of someone else hidden in the cracks of my soul,
like shadows you can't let go.
What if every smile you give me
is traced with memories of her laughter?
What if you see her reflection in my quiet moments,
or hear her name in the silence between my words?

Outside, the air was lighter,
her shoulders looser,
a quiet understanding settling between us.
As we stood, she reached for me,
held on longer than I expected.

For the first time, she saw herself in me,
not as a stranger,
but as someone she could become.

And as she walked away,
I hoped one day,
she would sit at this table again,
telling me all about the life
she once thought was impossible.

Life is not always about losing,
losing people you love,
losing memories,
losing moments that felt endless.
Loss is simply change in disguise,
a reminder that nothing stands still forever.
You cannot move through life untouched by it,
but you can choose to live in the moment,
to hold onto the here and now,
to love without fear of the ending.
Because in the end,
you will only lose what was never meant to stay,
but never your forever.

And it haunts me to this day,
why you didn't choose me.
Why it was so simple for you
to turn away,
to let go,
to never look back.

I don't care about your love for her,
about the battles fought behind closed doors.
I care that you never fought for me.
That you never stayed.
That you never chose
the one life sent to you,
the one who waited,
the one who wondered
what was so wrong with being yours.

My State of Felicity

Sometimes I want to drown my dreams,
let them sink beneath the weight of doubt,
watch them fade with the tide of my fears.

Because they seem too far away,
like distant stars I'll never touch,
like whispers lost in the wind.

Because I feel too small,
too fragile,
too uncertain to ever reach them.

But even as the waves rise,
somewhere deep inside,
a part of me still holds on,
a part of me still believes.

Angelina Schreiber

Maybe I am hard to love,
hard to keep,
hard to cherish.

Maybe I was never enough,
not for you to stay,
not for your feelings to grow into something real.

And maybe that's okay.
Because I have learned to be my own home,
to find love in my own reflection,
to hold myself when no one else will.

I was never taught how to be easy to love,
but I have always known how to love myself.

There was a time before you,
when my heart knew only its own rhythm,
unaware of the way yours would sync with mine.

And there will be a time after you,
when the ache of missing you will fade,
and I'll find new melodies to dance to,
new stories to write,
and new dreams to chase.

Angelina Schreiber

Break me, burn me, light me up,
Because you gave me the power to shine.

My State of Felicity

Angelina Schreiber

My State of Felicity
The making of

Exactly three years ago, I was sitting in my childhood bedroom at my parents' house, staring anxiously at my laptop. My very first book had just become available to everyone, and with that, I had fulfilled a dream I never thought would actually come true. I still remember how I dug out my old diary and checked off the very first item on my bucket list. I had done it. Tears rolled down my face, and I didn't quite know how to handle all of the emotions inside me.

Messages started pouring in, from friends, from family. Screenshots of book orders, texts saying how incredibly proud they were of me.

My State of Felicity isn't just a book. It was a dream. A dream and a collection of poems I used to secretly scribble into notebooks. My State of Felicity was my proof that I can achieve anything I set my mind to. That it doesn't matter what anyone else says, and that no dream is ever too small. With this book, I opened a door that had always been inside my heart. I just didn't know how to unlock it until then.

I always wanted to use my voice, my experiences, everything I went through, the good and the bad. Early on, people started asking how many books I'd sold or how much money I'd made. But that never mattered to me. From day one, I knew: if just one person bought my book, read my poems, felt understood, and said that my words helped them, then I had done everything right. Then this book was exactly where it was meant to be. Then every single letter in it had a purpose.

I was 20 when I wrote and published this book, and when I read the poems now, they still bring tears to my eyes. I knew so little, and yet so much. I've grown. I've gotten lost. I've found myself again. I've let people go. I've met new ones. And I never stopped writing. In every stage of life, I found words, during fresh starts, breakups, new perspectives. And I will never stop.

This is a life that was always meant to be lived this way.
And this is a dream that will keep going. Forever.

My State of Felicity